TOP DAWG

MARK RICHT AND THE REVIVAL OF GEORGIA FOOTBALL

ROB SUGGS

THOMAS NELSON

Since 1798

NASHVILLE   DALLAS   MEXICO CITY   RIO DE JANEIRO   BEIJING

Published in Nashville, Tennessee by Thomas Nelson. Thomas Nelson is a registered trademark of Thomas Nelson, Inc.

Published in association with the literary agency of Mark Sweeney & Associates, Bonita Springs, Florida 34135.

Thomas Nelson, Inc. titles may be purchased in bulk for educational, business, fund-raising, or sales promotional use. For information, please e-mail SpecialMarkets@ThomasNelson.com.

Library of Congress Cataloging-in-Publication Data

ISBN: 978-1-4016-0433-2

Printed in the United States of America

08 09 10 11 12 QW 5 4 3 2 1

CONTENTS

FOREWORD

I was excited when Rob Suggs asked me to write down a few words about a place and a person whom I love: the University of Georgia and Coach Mark Richt.

So much of who I am today came from five years of my life that were spent in Athens, Georgia. Those were five seasons I'll never forget.

First of all, there's the value of an education from the University of Georgia. My degree in speech communication means more to me than anything I've ever earned. No matter what else I might accomplish in my life, I will be proud of that diploma and all that it symbolizes.

Then there is the privilege of being a Georgia Bulldog. People ask me why I was willing to wait several years for one season as a starting quarterback. I tell them I have never regretted that decision—not for one moment. You see, I was the one who was blessed by being there. I stayed because of my teammates and because of Mark Richt. They did so much for me, and I wanted to do the same for them.

You have to understand how I feel about my teammates, my coach, my school. If you've ever walked across the campus and stepped into our locker room, you understand. If you've laced up your cleats to run onto that field at Sanford Stadium, with ninety-two thousand fans cheering, you understand. The richness of that atmosphere and the power of that tradition overwhelm you, and you soak up every day and minute that you are fortunate enough to be a Georgia Bulldog.

The University of Georgia is like nowhere else on this earth. I think about a stadium packed with fans all in red, on their feet shouting for the Dawgs, and I get juiced all over again. I think about the feeling of a Saturday night between the hedges with a game on the line, and I'm ready to suit up again! Ask any of us who were fortunate enough to wear the helmet with the big G—Bulldogs for life, that's who we are.

We're family, too. My coaches and teammates were my life while I was in Athens. Coach Richt was always honest with me, always a true man whom I respected to the fullest. Whenever I needed him, he was there for me, just as he was for everyone. It's no secret that Coach Richt is a fine human being and that his life is full to the brim with good works that he does for others. But he also instills discipline and dedication in every single player on his roster. He demands the very best of everyone who is around him, and because of that, we learn to demand the best of ourselves.

I love Coach Richt because he didn't just settle for helping us play football. He prepared us for the world that is outside the stadium. He showed us through the way he lived, the way he coached, and the way he cared, that there is so much more to being a man than just playing a game. I can honestly say that I am who I am today because of five years in the greatest environment on the face of this earth.

That's why I'm glad this story is being told. I look forward to reliving my days in the red and black, and feeling that Athens kind of adrenalin pumping through my veins again. It would be a great story, and I would still want to read it, even if it were just about football. But it's about so much more. Rob's book is all about striving to be the very best—how Mark Richt has done that, how the Georgia Bulldogs are doing that, and how you can do it, too.

One other thing . . .

Go Dawgs!

—D. J. Shockley
Atlanta Falcons
April 2008

INTRODUCTION

When I was six years old, my family moved from Georgia to Alabama. It's sad but true.

Family lore holds that my dad never set his watch "backward" to Central Time. He did take me to see my first Georgia game at Auburn, in 1962. Georgia won, 30–21, for one of its three victories of that season.

I knew as much about football as I did about nuclear fusion then, but I thought Auburn's song was very cool: "War Eagle, Fly Down the Field." I walked around our house humming it and told my dad I was now an Auburn fan. Aghast, he accelerated his efforts to get his children back to the state of Georgia. As we were packing the last boxes during Christmas of 1963, we heard news that Vince Dooley—another guy who had only imagined Auburn was cool—was also on his way to the promised land.

I resumed my growing-up process under the full and intoxicating influence of Georgia Bulldog football. My older brother and I would slip away just before halftime and stand around the fieldhouse, listening to Vince and Erk shout at the players inside, then staring up at their godlike presences as they stepped out for a cigarette.

I watched the Dawgs win championships, and I sat in the freezing downpour when Tech whipped us 34–14 in 1974. I saw Herschel Walker seem to fall from the heavens with lightning in his tread and keep us from losing an

SEC game or championship for three euphoric years. Vince Dooley was my prophet, and Lewis Grizzard provided my Scripture.

Georgia football has been a scarlet thread that has woven its way through my life. I've measured out my years by its celebrations and dirges. Just as my youth was ending in my midtwenties, the truly great seasons seemed to end with it. I crept into middle age without having savored the sweet taste of a championship in some time, until this latest coaching change. My youngest brother and I formed a pact to go to all the road games instead of simply the home games and see what this new coach could get done. Knoxville and Atlanta, 2001; Tuscaloosa, Columbia, Auburn, and the two Domes, 2002—so many of the greatest thrills came on those road trips. That queasy middle-aged feeling somehow drained away.

Seven years is a good biblical number. It seemed to mark out the time that took Richt's program from the unsettled place where he found it, to the elite place where he has delivered it. Before the 2007 season, therefore, we began talking about this book with publishers. We described the demand that we expected, given that by the end of the 2007 season Georgia would most assuredly be knocking at the door of very big things for 2008. Trust us on this, we said.

Just as we sent out our book proposal to publishers, Georgia lost at home to South Carolina and then took a savage pummeling on the road in Knoxville. One publisher in Alabama sent a mocking rejection slip. Man, I hated Alabama, but it looked like the book project was dead.

Then a whole host of Bulldogs ran onto the field in Jacksonville and did their dance; a bunch of them ran out of a tunnel wearing black jerseys and destroyed a team from Alabama. I enjoyed that very much. Suddenly, it was January 2008, and we were second-ranked and right where I had promised we would be. Hey, I never doubted it.

I wanted my book to tell the story of these seven remarkable years and attempt to show how Richt and his staff transcended the distance from also-ran to all-powerful.

I knew I would need to tell the story of the games themselves. But I also wanted to go a little deeper and examine the basic foundation stones upon which this success was built. First, there had to be a chapter on Richt and his pilgrimage to the Georgia position. I then thought about Knoxville in 2001, the breakthrough moment. I would need to consider the strong leadership of Richt's coaching staff and the excellence of talent gathering via our recruiting machine. Finally, there were the elements of faith and character building, and the sincere commitment of instilling them in our players.

I hope this book tells that story as accurately and fully as possible, and that it helps to document seven glorious years in the life of Georgia Bulldog football.

I would be remiss if I didn't thank the people who have helped me get this book—my dream project—in print. That begins with my agent, Mark Sweeney, who worked so hard to get this idea before the right publishers. I want to thank my whole family—particularly my father, who raised me up as a Bulldog, and my brother Joe, who got me to all those road games beginning in 2001—enduring memories. Pamela Clements, Geoffrey Stone, and Damon Goude at Thomas Nelson have been supportive and enthusiastic. Mike Towle has been a vigilant editor. Radi Nabulsi and the Florida State University athletic department provided terrific photographs. I want to give special thanks to Shelton Stephens, Charlie Norris, Justin Reynolds, D. J. Shockley, Greg Jarvis, "LowIQ," Kevin Hynes, Ann Hunt, Connie Connelly, Steve Patterson, Rodney Garner, and, of course, Coach Richt, who was insistent that this be a book about the Georgia Bulldogs and not about himself. It's not his book in any way; that story remains to be told someday. Even so, he was kind enough to give permission for us to use material from his Christian testimony and to grant interviews that were extremely helpful.

This book is lovingly dedicated to all the men who have coached for the University of Georgia throughout the years, and to their dedication and perseverance. They have gifted us joy, inspiration, and a sense of wonderful community that invariably becomes a defining legacy for our children.

—ROB SUGGS
April 2008

o 1 o

THE CHECKERBOARD STATEMENT

KNOXVILLE, 2001

"Men, you can make history today."

Mark Richt let that sentence soak in, one more time. He scanned the faces in the locker room, looking for confidence and intensity. If they were going to steal a win in Knoxville on October 6, 2001, these Bulldogs would have to find something new, something relentless within themselves and within each other.

Was that something there? Since January, Richt and his staff had spent a fair amount of time with this group of young men. In September, Georgia had won one and lost one in conference play, defeating Arkansas but losing a game in the final moments to South Carolina. Which result suggested the truth about these Bulldogs—the victory or the defeat?

The new head coach wasn't completely sure. The staff and the players were still taking each other's measure. Since winter conditioning, the team had been pushed to its limit in a boot camp atmosphere designed to instill toughness and togetherness. But it wasn't yet clear that the team had bought into the new ways of doing things. This season could go in one direction or the other. Transition years are difficult even in the best of circumstances.

Yet Richt had full confidence that good things were going to happen sooner or later. Maybe sooner—he was an optimist by nature. And at this moment, he felt a certain electricity in the stillness of the room, in the intensity of the eyes that met his.

From overhead came the muffled roar of one-tenth of a million adrenalin-spiked football fans, most of them ravenous for a Tennessee victory. Richt pointed toward the doorway and the field. In his typically placid tone, he continued to speak: "The last time any Georgia Bulldogs got a victory out there, some of you weren't even born. You know what year that was?"

Some of them mumbled the answer: *1980*. It was a year whose facts were drilled into every new Georgia player: Herschel Walker and the undefeated national champions—twenty-one long football seasons ago. For these players it was once-upon-a-time stuff.

"Men, twenty-one years is a long time. But you can do something about it today. Just stay focused. Execute. Take care of your assignment for one play, then do it again on the next one. We've got a good game plan; let's believe in it and carry it out."

It was a lot to ask for a football team under full renovation. Coach Jim Donnan, Richt's predecessor, had left a roster stocked with NFL-capable talent. Still, the coaching staff was new, the season was young, and everyone was learning the new rules. Today would bring the first test outside the comfort of Sanford Stadium in Athens.

The new staff would make its road debut under the following conditions:

- Tennessee would enter the game ranked sixth nationally; Georgia hadn't cracked the Top 25.

- Wide receiver Reggie Brown, injured the previous week against Arkansas, would miss the game as well as the rest of the season.

- Linebackers: Will Witherspoon would miss the next few games, Ryan Fleming was out with a knee injury, and Boss Bailey was playing with a broken hand in a cast.

- This injury-ridden linebacker corps would be called upon to stop Travis Stephens, one of the nation's most physical and durable running backs. He was capable of forty carries and of personally wearing down a defense.

- Tennessee had more than its share of injuries on both sides of the ball, but the roster was deep and talented.

- Georgia's quarterback, David Greene, would be a freshman also facing his first road game, in a hostile venue with 107,000 aggressively boisterous fans.

- While Georgia had accumulated three sacks, Tennessee already had ten.

- Georgia had made Arkansas quarterback Zak Clark, a 30 percent passer, look like an all-star. Yet Tennessee's Casey Clausen had last week lit up LSU for 309 yards—256 of them to phenomenal newcomer Kelley Washington.

- Decent and recent Georgia teams (including one that had beaten Florida by 20 points) had been overwhelmed and dominated in their last two appearances in Knoxville. That memory rested vividly inside the heads of the Bulldog upperclassmen.

- Georgia's kick coverage, which had given up touchdown returns in each of its two league games, offered a dangerous opening for Tennessee.

- The Volunteer defense was giving up all of 41 yards per game rushing.

- CBS planned to show the game to a national audience. Tennessee, wanting to impress the pollsters, was ready for its close-up.

There was no way to add up those factors and arrive at an encouraging total. Richt and his assistants recognized a zero-sum situation. Georgia had to play at a level it hadn't yet shown. The inconsistency of the previous games would mean disaster in Knoxville with the football world watching.

On the other hand—and here is what the coaches had to preach—the tougher the challenge, the more brilliant the prize. To be the best, you must beat the best. If the Georgia Bulldogs wanted to reclaim their place among the nation's elite, they needed to show proof, and this game was Exhibit A.

With all these things at stake, Tennessee Week began.

Monday's practice was less than inspiring. It's a common problem coming off a weekend, but on this occasion, excuses were unacceptable. The coaches wanted to optimize every detail of preparation for the game in Knoxville, and they pushed the players as hard as they had since mat drills, the torturous off-season endurance regimen. And they got a bit of a boost from unexpected quarters.

Every college team has a small squad of unsung heroes known as walk-ons. These student-athletes receive no financial scholarship and usually no playing time in games, but they show up on the practice field to help the team prepare. They're football's equivalent of the sparring partner in boxing, the guy who stands in the ring and takes a beating from the genuine contender.

Many walk-on players are used on the scout team, the unit that mimics the upcoming opponent in practice. Early in the week, one of them bought some orange adhesive tape and fashioned his helmet into a reasonable facsimile of the Tennessee Volunteer headgear. He then announced his intention to do everything in his power to "piss off the offense." He would even get into their faces, talk trash in hillbilly dialect, and grab the wide receivers illegally.

The idea caught on. Soon the rest of the scout team was busy at work creating UT helmets and taunting the offense. Richt chuckled, deciding it wasn't a bad idea at all. Some of the offensive players were losing their temper, delivering an extra blow to the Vol surrogates after the whistle (usually a common occurrence anyway). All to the good—angry practices make for angry execution on game day.

Richt held a practice in Sanford Stadium and piped in crowd noise and the music of the Tennessee marching band playing its fight song, "Rocky Top," over and over. The stadium sound system was maxed out so that the music and shouting were audible for miles. Students stood on the bridge beside the stadium, trying to catch a glimpse of the practice. As for the players, they couldn't hear anything but the music. Richt wouldn't allow

4

them to speak. They worked on communicating their signals visually, by hand, on both sides of the ball.

The players knew that nobody was giving them a shot in this game, and that's a time-tested motivation in itself. ESPN's Rece Davis wrote, "Tennessee is giving up a yard and a half per carry on defense. They are just too much for Georgia right now. Tennessee wins the game 34–14." Tony Barnhart of the *Atlanta Journal-Constitution* saw Tennessee winning by 14. And the same paper's Jeff Schultz, having some fun with what he called "ChihuahuaNation," wrote, "No upset this year. Take the [Vols], give the 11½. Arf."

The annual battle of the bulletin board also had to be waged. On Monday, Tennessee's freshman running back Jabari Davis, from Atlanta's Tucker High School, said that he chose Tennessee because "Georgia was always talking about getting to the Peach Bowl. Here, we're not talking about the Peach Bowl. We're talking about going to the Rose Bowl." He was alluding to the Rose Bowl as an occasional national championship site.

Proud Georgia fans predictably took umbrage. Richt, declining to take the bait, said that he thought the jibe was humorous. "Freshman," summarized offensive tackle Jon Stinchcomb, rolling his eyes.

Before Davis's remark could be dutifully tacked to the Bulldog bulletin board, Greene, of all people, provided ammunition for the other side. When asked about the challenge of playing his first road game in Knoxville, Greene said, "I've heard it's a tough place to play, but I've heard it's overrated, too."

The battle of words, fought by freshmen, ended in a tie; the real battle, the one fought on grass and gridiron, was ready to commence.

ROCKY TOP, ROCKY START

Richt took one more look at his troops before leading them onto the Knoxville field. "If they blow the doors off us early, keep your composure," he advised. "Believe in the plan. Now let's get out there and finish the drill, men."

Everyone stood up, and there was the metal pop of scores of chin guards snapping to helmets. Then everyone gathered around the door, and you could hear the rising din of eighty-five student-athletes marshalling their battle spirits. Some shouted, some simply gritted their teeth, many were profane, but every man reached deep into his own personal psyche and summoned the emotional fuel he needed. Jumping up and down, restless for contact, the team moved into the tunnel and waited for the signal.

Then, just like that, they were emerging from the shadow and onto the bright field of battle. The younger ones were struck by the sheer noise level of the nation's second-largest sports venue. You can be told about it, you can practice with crowd noise over the speakers all you like, and you can prepare yourself mentally; you still won't be ready for the shock of 107,000 feverish, bellowing spectators surrounding you on every front while the band plays "Rocky Top" over and over.

Besides, if you know your team is a work in progress while the other coach is 51–4 on these premises, your full measure of intestinal fortitude had better be present and accounted for. The coaches and players believed, hoped, hungered.

There had been rain early in the morning, and a few clouds remained, but it was becoming a nice enough day. At noon, kickoff time, the temperature was holding steady at fifty degrees. Tennessee won the toss, deferred its possession option to the second half, and kicked off to the visitors.

And instantly, Greene, who had wondered about the intimidation factor in Neyland Stadium, was leading his offense onto the field to find out.

Early events seemed to confirm the wisdom of the pundits. On first down, Greene had to divest himself of the ball under pressure of stampede. On second down, Terence Edwards dropped a pass as he absorbed a percussive collision. A third-down pass completion came up short.

Three and out, and Georgia had been too timid even to attempt a handoff. The crowd thundered its approval.

Tennessee then took the ball and submitted a showcase touchdown drive—Tennessee power football at its most imposing. Clausen handed the ball to Stephens repeatedly, and Stephens shed tacklers like old sweaters. He finally broke into the open field and looked a cinch to go the distance, until he stumbled over his own feet at the Georgia 7.

It was only a momentary stay of execution for the Bulldogs. Kelley Washington caught a touchdown, one foot in bounds, in the left end zone over double coverage. The score stood at 7–0, and the Tennessee bench was visibly relaxed, laughing, enjoying its afternoon. After one possession for each team, no one could have mistaken which squad was the national contender and which was the pretender.

After freshman Fred Gibson returned the kickoff to the 43, the Dawgs acquitted themselves well. Musa Smith rushed twice for a first down. Ben Watson caught one pass for 9. Labrone Mitchell ran a slant route to perfection and the 18-yard line. This was a vast improvement over the first brief possession. But Tennessee became tougher in the shadow of its own goalpost; the drive stalled, and Billy Bennett kicked a field goal. Tennessee 7, Georgia 3.

As the first quarter progressed, the Bulldogs seemed to be taking the coach's advice. UT had "blown off the doors" just as he had warned, but the Georgia team refused to lose its composure. The defense discovered it could make a stop, and the offense was picking up confidence—until the moment when the freshman portion of Greene made its first appearance. He forced a terrible throw into coverage over the middle of the field, and Tennessee's Rashad Baker took the ball out of the air on a full sprint. He returned it to the Georgia 17, and Clausen hit Leonard Scott for an easy touchdown pass on the next play.

Now it was 14–3, with a feeling in the Georgia fan section that it could be a long day. The Bulldogs' challenge was tall enough without spotting the opposition gift touchdowns. It pumped up the crowd noise, encouraged the Vols, and put the Dawgs in a very treacherous position. Too often they'd done this very thing: come into Neyland and let the game get out of hand. Tennessee was looking loose, hungry, ready to bring down the hammer.

Yet once again, the Dawgs answered; once again they provided a clue that a new breed had replaced the old psychologically and physically intimidated Georgia Bulldogs. Gibson returned the ensuing kickoff 31 yards. Fullback Verron Haynes was isolated on a beautiful play-action fake and rambled for 29. Smith ran for 5, and then for a first down. Against a defense like Tennessee's, every yard on the ground was like gold, giving Greene the opportunity to work the passing game.

On third down, inside the 10-yard line, the referees called for a measurement; Georgia was about a foot short. Smith powered forward for what appeared to be a full yard, but another measurement was commissioned—and the Dawgs came up short.

This was a key moment in the game. The Bulldogs had bogged down after an impressive drive, settling for the field goal. This time everyone on the Georgia side was certain that Smith had picked up the necessary yardage and put his team in position for a touchdown. The team had another opportunity to be discouraged. It had been a tough drive, a physically exhausting one, and it ended with no points and a questionable measurement. But the defense "bowed its neck," as Richt liked to put it, and forced a Tennessee punt.

Damien Gary wasn't even supposed to be returning punts. Reggie Brown had that job, but he'd been lost for the season. Now, Gary fielded the kick, made a couple of lethal fakes in traffic, and suddenly had nothing but stripes in his field of vision. He sprinted toward the delighted, Georgia-dominated end zone, completing the school's first punt return touchdown in eight years. Finishing with the obligatory somersault into the end zone, he provoked a 15-yard celebration penalty that made the extra point a bit more adventurous than usual.

The effect on the Georgia bench was galvanizing—a quick charge of electricity that put every player on his feet screaming for Gary to run. This was the point when the most outlandish hope suddenly seemed within reach. Tennessee was bringing its usual power game and—what a concept—the Bulldogs were counterpunching. Neyland fell silent except for two factions: the Georgia bench, whooping and hollering, and the visiting Georgia fans, who were cramped within the league's smallest seats but bursting with fresh pride.

FIGHTING BACK

Gradually the Georgia defense began to believe in itself. The players refused to back down, increasing their intensity as they discovered they had a shot to take home a victory. Stephens began to go down behind the line or after modest gains, rather than imposing his will on the defense every play. Somehow the Dawgs began winning their share of battles along the front line. David Jacobs was having a career day; Tony Gilbert, one of the few truly healthy linebackers, seemed to participate in every tackle. Georgia had failed to measure up physically to recent Tennessee teams in Neyland. Now the players were beginning to believe they could stand toe-to-toe with their rivals.

On offense, Georgia was doing much of its damage with two weapons. Fullback Haynes seemed constantly open in the flat and capable of rambling down the sideline once he got the ball. Tight end Randy McMichael, on the other hand, never seemed open on his post and crossing routes—which made no difference as he pulled down highlight-reel catches, putting on a show for a CBS-TV national audience. The next time the Dawgs pulled into scoring position, Gibson found himself all alone in the middle on an underneath route, and he trotted easily into the end zone. Again, the touchdown was scored directly in front of the exhilarated visiting fan section. Having once been down by double digits, Georgia was suddenly leading by a field goal. How long could it last?

Not too long. Stephens could not be held in check forever. He escaped again for 64 yards, though Georgia managed to hold Tennessee to a tying field goal. The Vols had one more shot to take the lead before halftime, but Alex Walls missed a 34-yarder with twenty seconds left in the half.

It was a hopeful way to go into the locker room for intermission. The position coaches quietly reviewed assignments with their players, who gulped POWERADE, caught their breath, and realized they were part of something that could be special.

Richt sat down and counseled with Brian VanGorder. The question was whether to adjust for Stephens. Tennessee was on a pace to rush for nearly 300 yards for the day. The defense had adjusted and limited the damage for the most part, but there was the danger of simply wearing out, particularly with no health or depth at linebacker. Tennessee had held the ball for nineteen minutes to Georgia's eleven.

"Stay patient," said Richt. "Let's stick with the game plan. I think our guys are up to the challenge." The way to stop the ground game, of course, was to bring up the safeties. But that would mean isolating the cornerbacks in single-man coverage with UT's dangerous Washington and Scott. The previous week, LSU had tried that approach and lived to regret it. Washington had set a school record with 256 yards, eventually breaking loose on a long run that sealed the victory. Therefore it was a matter of naming your poison: death by Stephens's legs or Clausen's arm? Richt and VanGorder didn't want to gamble in either direction.

Cornerback Tim Wansley was rising to the challenge. He was on a mission, hounding Washington on every play. He was calling the receiver out, getting in his face and saying, "Not on me!" And he was backing up his talk by limiting the damage. But the Georgia coaches knew that if Wansley and Bruce Thornton were left in man coverage, the dam was going to break sooner or later.

VanGorder agreed to stick with two-deep pass coverage in the second half. Eight different players would be rotated on the defense—including freshmen like David Pollack—and they would simply have to step up and make plays. Richt was a game-plan guy: prepare your best strategy, commit to it, and stay calm and on task.

It was Richt's first great strategic test as a head coach. He was ready to put the headphones back on, work thirty more minutes on the clock, and see how it all came out.

ENDGAME

The third quarter had a clear theme, and that was field position. Kick coverage, which had seemed like a liability coming in, was achieving something remarkable. On two straight occasions, Jonathan Kilgo got the punt high in the air, and his coverage team had gotten downfield to down the ball at the 1-yard line. On the first of these, Wansley grabbed the ball and neatly dropped it thirty-six inches from the goal line as his body fell into the end zone.

As a result, Tennessee was running uphill all quarter. Backed up in his own territory with the score tied, Vol offensive coordinator Randy Sanders became even more conservative, staying with the running game. For the first time, a few boos emerged from the home crowd. On the other hand, Georgia couldn't do a thing with its superior field position. To its credit, Tennessee's injury-ridden defense stepped up and made plays.

The game was becoming a chess match, mostly played on the Tennessee side of the board. If you wore orange, you felt that Tennessee was gradually wearing its opponent down, slowly turning the field around, and preparing for a fourth-quarter kill. If you wore red, you were a bundle of nerves, but you just knew Georgia's big break was going to come at any second. And if you were neutral, you were sitting back and enjoying the show; this was one of the most intense football games you'd ever seen.

With eight minutes remaining in the game, Georgia got the ball at its own 12. Gibson came up on an underneath route, grabbed a pass, and sprinted 55 yards to the Tennessee 33. Running back Jasper Sanks carried the ball down to the 21. After a penalty, McMichael got the yardage back on a magnificent pass by Greene. Sanks took the ball to the 12, where there was another penalty against the Dawgs. It seemed as if nobody had scored for hours. Finally, with a little more than five minutes remaining, Bennett kicked a field goal to give Georgia the lead.

It was time for Tennessee to decide if it was going to win this game. Georgia's defense was winded. Was there anything left in the tank?

The Vols began to move, though Georgia's defensive backs were covering pass routes beautifully. That day they seemed to have grown up. With 1:53 left on the clock, Tennessee had managed to reach the outskirts of field goal territory. Georgia safety Jermaine Phillips leaped into the air and stole a pass over Bobby Graham. Georgia's fan section exploded. Could it really have happened? Was the game over?

The answers were yes and no, respectively. With the ball deep in its own territory, Georgia tried to milk the clock while Tennessee used all its time-outs in desperation. Again, Richt chose the conservative route: Execute, protect the ball, don't beat yourself by forcing a pass. Yet after three running plays, only twenty-one seconds had drained from the clock. In the immortal words of Bulldogs play-by-play announcer Larry Munson, "The clock just wouldn't move."

Tennessee sent its roster after Kilgo's punt and almost got a hand on it. The Vols began their final possession 79 yards from the end zone with 1:15 on the clock and no timeouts.

No one could have anticipated the extraordinary finales that both teams had reserved for this afternoon.

FINISHING THE DRILL

Tennessee appeared to have run out of luck. Washington dropped a pass with a little help from Phillips. Fleming caught his pass for a first down, but the Vols were still 63 yards from the end zone. Bailey nearly intercepted the next ball. It was time for Georgia to slam the door. The Bulldogs seemed to be sitting on every pass route.

Then Clausen tossed a screen pass to Stephens. Stephens broke free, but he didn't seem to have any extraordinary angle for a long run. What he did have was a gear he hadn't used yet, and he put down the stick and accelerated to it. Georgia's exhausted linebackers and defensive backs strained to overtake Stephens, but he sailed into the end zone.

Neyland erupted like a rocky mountain volcano. The noise level was nearly apocalyptic. This would be one of the great Volunteer wins, a 62-yard miracle play that saved the home team from disaster, preserving a national championship run. It would be an afternoon to tell the grandchildren about.

During the ear-splitting chaos, Richt registered no particular emotion on the Georgia sideline. "The headphones were outstanding," he said later with the slightest trace of a smile. He was already talking to Greene, already dipping back into the plan.

The game, which seemed like a multiseason epic by now, still had forty-two unused seconds and one unused miracle.

Tennessee squibbed the kickoff. There was much consternation about this decision afterward in the home locker room. The intent was to avoid a long return, but Georgia started on its own 40. The deficit was 4 points, so a field goal would be useless. Greene brought the team on the field with as calm a demeanor as his head coach. In the huddle there was a lot of insistent chatter.

"We're gonna do this!"

"Let's finish the drill."

"Let's get it done."

"Stay focused," said Greene. "There's plenty of time to win this thing."

Every man believed. The stadium was still erupting in invocations of support for the defense, but the Georgia players paid no attention. The coaches had told them there would be a moment like this. They were either going to claim their destiny as winners or they were going to stop believing in each other, give in, and accept defeat. The coaches had pushed them to the limit in mat drills months ago. They had made them run wind sprints until they were physically ill.

The team was ready to find out what the future held for Georgia football. Greene called for silence and gave out the play.

Gary lined up in the slot, took a pass from what Richt called an option route, broke a tackle, and took the ball to the Tennessee 47. On the next play, Greene rolled out to his right to avoid the murderous pass rush. But Tennessee's defense was flooding the routes, and no one was open. Greene threw incomplete.

The clock was down to 00:26. McMichael, tangled up in orange, somehow came down with a catch in the middle of the field, at the Tennessee 20.

The jubilant noise in the stadium began to subside. For the Vol faithful, this game against an inferior opponent had gone off script. It was becoming almost quiet enough to hear the clock tick off the seconds: 00:20, 00:19 . . .

McMichael turned up in yet another section of the field, snagging a pass at the 6-yard line—unthinkably close to the goal line. Could it be happening? The Georgia sideline was now in disarray, with players leaping up and down, pumping fists, shouting at the top of their lungs.

Ten seconds was a good round number, and Richt called time out.

On the sidelines, the head coach's hair was tousled, but his demeanor was unruffled. Greene listened attentively as Richt found the play he'd had in mind for this very situation.

P-44 HAYNES

It was dubbed P-44 Haynes, in honor of its primary target.

This was the kind of play designed to work against one type of coverage only. Richt had to assume the Vols were going to double up on the wide receivers and that they would also come after the quarterback. If the middle linebacker could be accounted for, a fullback could sneak up the middle and have a clear shot at the end zone.

Greene had to watch for Tennessee's defensive alignment. "If there is a single safety," Richt told the quarterback, "just throw it into the stands, and we'll have one more play. If there are two of them, we'll split the middle and throw it to Verron." It seemed a good bet that UT would use two safeties and assign each one to a side of the field, but it was important for Greene to identify the coverage. A single safety would play in the middle and spoil the call.

On the sidelines, Haynes was standing nearby as he heard Richt and Greene mention his name. For a moment he wasn't certain what play they were talking about. Then it hit him.

This was a play Richt had loved using at Florida State with "Pooh Bear" Williams at fullback. The play had been put in for the Bulldogs before the season, and Haynes naturally loved it. He had asked Greene several times when he would hear it called, so he could run up the middle and grab his easy pass. But Richt had never called it during the first three games, and Haynes had forgotten the whole thing.

Now, with a jolt, he realized he would get his shot at P-44 Haynes. It wasn't his job to account for safeties, block, or anything else. All he really had to do was keep his feet under him, dodge the middle linebacker, and turn around for the ball—and one other thing. *Hang on.*

As Greene called signals, he watched Tennessee reveal its scheme. Sure enough, it was "quarter coverage," meaning that the four defensive backs were splitting the field into four quadrants, and there would be a beautiful seam right up the middle. That meant P-44 Haynes had a chance to work.

Greene took the snap and faked a handoff to the running back. Haynes moved toward Keyon Whiteside, the onrushing linebacker, as if he were going to throw a block. At the last second, Haynes sidestepped Whiteside, took several steps forward, and found he was alone on the orange checkerboard—or perhaps it was a chessboard, because Richt had established a checkmate.

For the fullback, time seemed to move in slow motion, just like in a movie. The game clock ticked to 00:05 and simply seemed to stop. The brown pigskin, spinning in a perfect arc, seemed as big and round as a beach ball. Greene might have muffed the throw; Haynes might have muffed the catch. It was all simply too easy, considering the McMichael catches in heavy traffic.

Don't drop it, thought Haynes. *Do not drop it!*

But the ball slid perfectly into the fullback's desperate hands, and Haynes, who had been recruited only by I-AA Western Kentucky, who had transferred and walked on in Athens without a scholarship, who had sat out a season before carrying the ball ten times in two full seasons—Verron Haynes, obscure blue-collar fullback, joined the ranks of the legendary.

The Georgia bench dissolved into delirious chaos, with the exception of Richt, who was still playing chess. He signaled for no extra-point conversion. Meanwhile, Haynes sprinted toward the sideline, pounding his helmet with one fist and still cradling the ball in the other. No way he was going to drop that thing, even now. Wherever he is now, he still might be holding that ball.

Hardly anyone noticed the strange play that followed, because nearly everyone in attendance was either weeping or wailing or gnashing his or her teeth. Richt elected not to kick the point because of the risk involved. It was a 2-point game now, 26–24, and a blocked kick could be returned to the other end zone for precisely the value of a tie. And why not? By now every other conceivable miracle had transpired in this game.

Instead, Greene ran the "victory formation"—full protection with the quarterback kneeling to cradle the precious ball—and Georgia sat on the lead with five seconds remaining.

Georgia still had to execute one play, a kickoff to Tennessee. The Vols received, attempted a completely nonmiraculous lateral, and were smothered by one joyful army of Bulldogs.

Game over.

FACE-STEPPING AND FINISHING

Georgia's legendary radio announcer, Munson, was inspired to a kind of coarse, almost poetic, frenzy. "We just stepped on their face with a hobnail boot and broke their nose!" he shouted. For good measure, he added, "We just crushed their face!"

Meanwhile, Richt was making his way to the middle of the field to shake the hand of Tennessee's head coach Phil Fulmer. Then he jogged over toward the Georgia fan section and saluted the faithful who had stayed on their feet and shouted the minority opinion until their voices were gone. The fans saluted him back—with the remains of their vocal cords.

Richt, the coaches, and the team enjoyed a wild celebration in the locker room. The Georgia football program had found its point of convergence. No longer was there any question that the team had bought into the new leadership. From that day forward, coaches and players alike always noted that this was the moment when it all came together. The pieces fit: the mat drills, the boot camp preseason, all the tension that results from a new staff inheriting an established team.

The coaches had talked about "finishing the drill" until everyone was sick of the phrase. They had preached the doctrine of hanging tough in the fourth quarter when a game was won or lost; about the full year of conditioning that is required so a man can rise up to prevail in those brief, grueling moments two or three times a season in the games that separate the elite teams from the rest of the pack.

They had finished the mat drills. They had played as hard as they could possibly play against South Carolina, and none of it had worked. The Gamecocks, a team that Georgia had once owned, finished that drill. But now, with this final, shocking drive against the sixth best team in the nation, every Bulldog understood what those words meant, where this program was going, and how good it felt to come through the fire as the victor.

Before every game, as the team does its calisthenics on the field, it eventually circles around the head coach at the 25-yard line. He leads them in a "breakdown" drill in which they follow his rapid commands, touching helmet, then thigh pads. After this game, when Richt trotted into the Knoxville locker room, he started the breakdown drill again, and all the players took part just as they would before a game. It was a unique bonding moment between coach and team. It was as if, though they'd performed this drill many times with him before, now the union was complete. "Breakdown" meant breaking down the walls, breaking down the resistance to new ways of being a team and a winning program. The Georgia Bulldogs had become more than a team. Now they were family.

Richt called out, "Did we finish the drill?"

The team shouted their answer in the affirmative.

"Did we stand together like brothers?"

The team shouted again.

Richt said a few more words, poured out his heart, and then it got crazy. Coach Jon Fabris broke into an amazing solo dance. The players circled around him, laughing for all they were worth. Those who were there claim that even Vince Dooley showed a couple of nifty steps. That day, anything was possible. Later, Dooley said, "We haven't had a game like this in a very long time."

True. But it was also beyond question that there would be more of these to come, and this time the wait would not be so long.

No historical distance was required to understand what was taking place. You could feel it that very moment in a Knoxville locker room. Dawn had broken for the Georgia football program. It was the beginning of a new day.

the rounds and checked out the athletes, his eye fell upon this gifted, athletic baseball player. He issued the kid a challenge that seemed to come right out of left field.

"You handle the glove pretty well," he said. "You can hit for power. But after you get to be eighteen years old and you graduate, what's next? Concentrate on football, son, and I can show you how to turn your skills into a full ride in college."

The words stopped Richt in his tracks. Like most tenth graders, he honestly hadn't thought much about the future. But there was something compelling about this new football coach; you almost couldn't help but follow Coffey.

Soon Richt found himself a regular guest in the coach's home, watching film, staring at scribbled "X"s and "O"s on pads of paper at the kitchen table, learning about the intricacies of this football thing. There was a whole *mental* game here, a strategy element that was invigorating. Coffey trained him to think like a quarterback. And that position—well, it seemed like the ultimate in sports competition. You could run. You could pass. You could be the unquestioned leader. Even a pitcher—commanding the mound in baseball— couldn't measure up to the adrenaline rush of taking charge of a huddle under the Friday-night lights. A quarterback could be "the man," no doubt about it. And so it came to be that Mark Richt, high school athlete, committed his heart and soul to football and the Boca Raton Bobcats.

By his junior year, NCAA Division I schools came calling. Richt began thinking more about his future. It seemed logical that he would be just as successful in college ball as he had been in high school, and then he would go on to the NFL and play on Sundays.

There were unexpected trials, of course. First he learned about the body part that "nature never meant for football"—the human knee. He went down with a painful injury and missed most of his junior year. He knew he would heal and get back onto the field. Everything pointed toward his senior year—that was payoff time, when he would show the world what he could do.

Then, just before his big autumn, Coach Coffey was asked to leave. The school brought in another man, Otis Gray. This was Richt's moment in the spotlight. He had never considered that his mentor might not share the glory with him. Richt quickly organized a players' meeting at his home, hoping to circulate a petition, attract attention, do whatever it took to retrieve his beloved football coach.

Coffey was gone. Eventually Richt accepted and respected his new coach and had a big senior year. He made First Team All-State at his position, and his mentor had been right: he could pick and choose where to receive a free education and a chance to play in huge stadiums and ABC's *Game of the Week*.

EYE OF A HURRICANE

Richt received a number of scholarship offers, but his final choice was to stay close to his home in Boca Raton by signing with the University of Miami.

Today, *Miami Hurricanes* is a name that brings to mind success and dominance. In the late 1970s it was not so. The program was mired in mediocrity, and there were rumblings about discontinuing the sport entirely. Lou Saban, the legendary NFL coach and cousin of Alabama's Nick Saban, had shown reasonable progress in 1977 and '78, but he had moved on. The next coach needed to get the job done, or Miami football would be in trouble. Lou Saban's successor, Howard Schnellenberger, would come from the NFL, where he had been a protégé of Don Shula with the Baltimore Colts.

Richt felt that his future was set. He would arrive on campus just in time for a new era. The buzz was that Schnellenberger was bringing the pro attack to college, a wide-open passing game that could bewilder Miami's run-based opponents. Coffey had trained Richt for a more sophisticated approach to football like this one—something more than handing off the ball for 3 yards and a cloud of dust. In 1979, college football was still the domain of the running back. Schnellenberger's strategy was more about the signal caller—and that suited Richt just fine.

As an eighteen-year-old, Richt had a game plan for life that was elegant in its simplicity. As he often tells it today, he would make his entrance as a freshman by starting at quarterback. He would be a consensus All-American as a sophomore and then win the Heisman Trophy as a junior. He would have to be patient, naturally, since early entrance to the draft for the National Football League wasn't an option until the 1980s. Therefore he would use his senior year to set passing records and await his first-round selection in the NFL draft. No one could say the All-State kid from Boca Raton didn't set high goals for himself.

As he moved onto the Coral Gables campus in late summer of 1979, one of the first players he met was another quarterback. Redshirt freshman Jim Kelly had come all the way from East Brady, Pennsylvania. How had he escaped the clutches of Joe Paterno and the Penn State Nittany Lions? It happened by a piece of adept recruiting finesse by Lou Saban, who was casting his net wide. Penn State didn't want Kelly at quarterback; the way JoePa saw it, Kelly was too good an athlete to be wasted at that position. Penn State had a reputation to uphold as a factory for NFL linebackers— LBU. "Join the Lions and be a run-stopper," he offered.

Saban visited Kelly's home. He drew up NFL passing plays on a napkin and made a counteroffer: "Come to Miami and help us build QBU."

That's precisely what happened for 1980s Miami football, though Saban would not be there for the fulfillment of his prophecy. Kelly would start a run of talent that included Bernie Kosar, Vinny Testaverde, Steve Walsh, Craig Erickson, and Gino Torretta.

Richt couldn't have come at a better time to watch the building of a quarterback (and championship) factory; he simply had to take it sitting down, from the vantage point of the bench. In a sense, he was in the eye of the Hurricane. Later he would look at these events and comprehend them as God shaping a future head coach; he certainly didn't have the benefit of that perspective as a college student-athlete.

While Richt was looking for playing time, he took in other things he wasn't necessarily seeking. For example, he observed how a new coach took a mediocre program and began changing its culture and mind-set. Schnellenberger was a public relations wizard, tirelessly visiting the off-season fan gatherings and talking to them about national championships. Miami fans, who had been discussing dropping football, shook their heads at such boldness.

Current players such as Art Kehoe, who remained as a Miami assistant coach for years, commented on how Schnellenberger reached out to the upperclassmen who were attached to Saban. This was something Richt had experienced as a high school senior. Schnellenberger built a bridge from the past to a more successful future by embracing Miami tradition (what there was of it) and implanting pride in the privilege of wearing green and orange.

Not that Howard was an old softy. As the Hurricanes were to discover, he had coached not only under Shula, but also under Bear Bryant. He knew all about training camps that seemed like boot camps. He understood the importance of conditioning and what it meant to be sufficiently football-tough to win championships. His first summer session with the players in Coral Gables was a very demanding one.

The education of an eighteen-year-old future coach included these elements: bringing in a proficient passing attack; implanting toughness and conditioning; creating a sense of school pride, *esprit de corps*, and the embracing of tradition; and making tough personnel decisions without looking back.

Most of these things are standard to some extent, but they are particularly critical emphases with Richt.

LUCKY JIM

Richt got along well with Jim Kelly, who won his coveted starting position. The two players were both born in February 1960, only four days apart. With his typical self-effacing humor, Richt would later describe the competition that went on in practice. It seemed to him that he would do everything right, memorize the playbook, hit perfect passes, but the ball would bounce out of the receivers' hands and into those of the cornerback. "Lucky Jim," as he called Kelly, just had everything work right for him on the field.

For his part, Kelly called Richt "Boca Baby." (To Richt's relief, the embarrassing nickname was shortened to "Boca" when the two touched base years later.)

"To this day," said Richt, "there are two people who still believe I was a better quarterback than Jim Kelly: my mother and me." He uses self-effacing humor when describing his athletic fortunes. But on the inside, Richt wasn't laughing back in 1979. He was overwhelmed by the challenges of the competition at this level as opposed to the local high school game.